ARKANSAS

A Turner Educational Services, Inc. book. Based on the Portrait of America television series created by R.E. (Ted) Turner.

Library of Congress Number: 87-16372

Library of Congress Cataloging in Publication Data

Thompson, Kathleen.
   Arkansas.

   (Portrait of America)
   "A Turner book."
   Summary: Discusses the history, economy, culture, and future of Arkansas. Also includes a state chronology, pertinent statistics, and maps.
   1. Arkansas—Juvenile literature. [1. Arkansas]
I. Title. II. Series: Thompson, Kathleen.
Portrait of America.
F411.3.T48   1987   976.7   87-16372

ISBN 0-8174-449-4   hardcover library binding

ISBN 0-8114-6770-8   softcover binding

Cover Photo: Arkansas Department of Parks and Tourism

      4 5 6 7 8 9 0   96 95 94 93 92 91

★ ★ ★ ★ ★
Portrait of AMERICA

ARKANSAS

Kathleen Thompson

RAINTREE
STECK-VAUGHN
L I B R A R Y
A Division of Steck-Vaughn Company

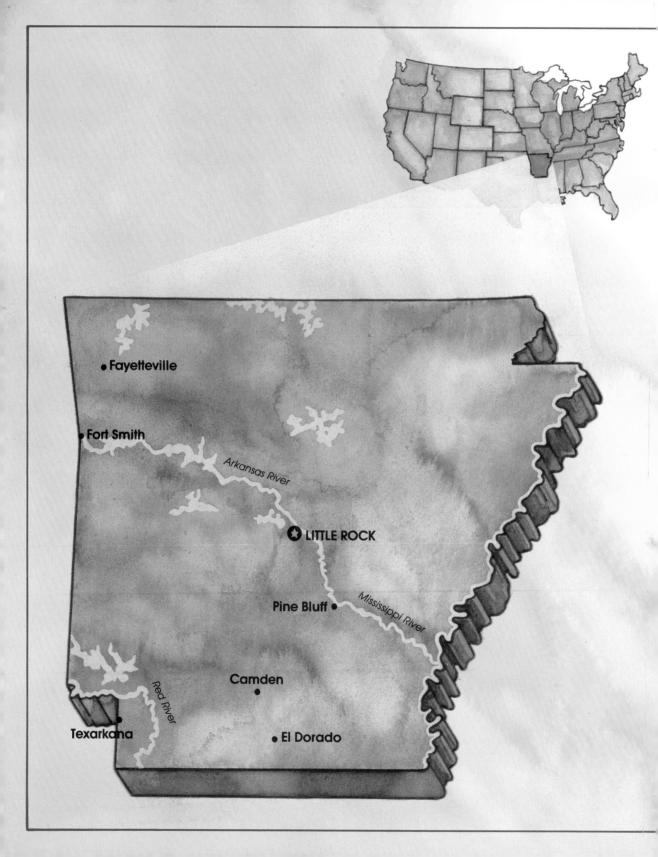

Fayetteville

Fort Smith

Arkansas River

★ LITTLE ROCK

Pine Bluff

Mississippi River

Camden

Red River

Texarkana

El Dorado

CONTENTS

Introduction

Arkansas, Land of Opportunity.

"You cross the Missouri line, it's totally different. You go to Oklahoma, you go to Kansas, it's different. You gotta get to this little corner in northwest Arkansas, and it just blooms."

Arkansas: cotton, forests, the Ozarks, caverns, rice, refrigerators, the future.

"It was not a place for a black, urban young woman to go. My family felt I would not fit in; I'd be most unhappy. Nevertheless, I'm still here; and I'm very happy."

Tucked between Mississippi and Tennessee to the east, Oklahoma and Texas to the west, Louisiana to the south, and Missouri to the north, Arkansas is the smallest state west of the Mississippi River. It has in it something of the West and something of the South. It is a place of sometimes breathtaking beauty and sometimes heartbreaking poverty. But it is always a place of strength and courage and determination.

A Long Way to Little Rock

Nomadic hunters, the Paleo-Indians, roamed through Arkansas as early as 10,000 B.C. The first natives of Arkansas hunted in its thick forests and farmed on its rich plains. They lived on the bluffs or cliffs, and their culture lasted between 8,000 and 1,000 B.C. Because of where they lived, they were called Bluff Dwellers.

From 1300-1700, people called Mound Builders filled the area. Like the Aztecs of South America and the ancient Egyptians, they built huge monuments to their dead. They also made fine pottery, decorations, and arrowheads.

By the time the first Europeans entered the region in the sixteenth century, Arkansas belonged to the Caddo, Osage, Quapaw, Cherokee, and Choctaw Indians.

A Spanish explorer, Hernando de Soto, came to Arkansas

A painting of the early explorations of Arkansas

in 1541. He looked around but then left. More than 125 years would pass before the next Europeans came. There was that much more time for the Caddo, Osage, Quapaw, Cherokee, and the Choctaw to hunt, fish, and farm the land.

But in 1673, two explorers came down the Mississippi River from Canada. They were Father Jacques Marquette and Louis Jolliet, and it was their task to follow the Mississippi to its source. They were in the service of France. A few years later because of French explorations, Robert Cavelier, Sieur de la Salle, claimed the entire Mississippi Valley for France.

This area, which the French called Louisiana after their king, was huge. It was made up of all the land where the rivers drained into the Mississippi, including Arkansas. Of course, no one bothered to ask the people who lived on the land what they thought about a French king declaring that he owned it.

In 1686, Henri de Tonti built a camp at the mouth of the Arkansas River. It was the first permanent European settlement in what would become Arkansas. Arkansas Post, as it was called, was used as a way station for travelers between the Gulf of Mexico and the Great Lakes. It was also a trading post for fur trappers.

Still, life was little changed for the people who lived in Arkansas. The French were interested in the new world primarily for its resources, not for settling and colonizing. One colony (founded by the Western Company) tried to develop the resources of the area, but it failed. Most of the colonists left. Another colony, made up of German farmers this

Marquette University, Milwaukee

On the left-hand page is Jacques Marquette. Fur trading was an important part of Arkansas history. A reenactment is shown above.

time, was started in 1720. It failed, too.

In 1763, France lost the Louisiana Territory to Spain. In 1783, the Spanish began to allow Americans to settle in Arkansas. However, the French won the land back in 1800. And in 1803, Napo-

leon found himself involved in some expensive wars. To get money, he offered to sell the Louisiana Territory to the United States for a ridiculously low price. Thomas Jefferson bought it. Arkansas now belonged to the United States, and the days of peace were over for its Indian people.

In 1812, the Louisiana Territory was split up. The southern part of the region became the state of Louisiana. The northern part became the Missouri Territory. In 1819, the Arkansas Territory was formed. It included Arkansas and part of what is now Oklahoma. Because of the Missouri Compromise, the Arkansas Territory was created as a place where slavery was allowed.

By the time Arkansas became a state seventeen years later, Congress had taken all the land in Arkansas away from the Osage, Quapaw, Caddo, Cherokee, and Choctaw. They were forced to move west into the Indian Territory (now Oklahoma). Most of them did not live to see their new home.

By 1860, there were more than four hundred thousand people

11

living in Arkansas and more than one hundred thousand of them were slaves. When Abraham Lincoln was elected president in 1861, southern states began to withdraw from the Union. They formed the Confederacy.

Arkansas was a slave state, but its people were divided in their feelings. Many people in the northern part of the state wanted to remain in the Union. A convention was called in March of 1862 to decide what the state should do. That convention voted to stay in the Union. But when Lincoln called for troops to fight against the Confederacy, the convention met again. This time

Arkansas withdrew, nearly a month after the Civil War had begun.

Still, about six thousand men from Arkansas joined the Union Army. About fifty-eight thousand fought for the Confederacy.

In 1863, the Union troops captured Little Rock, the state capital. The Confederates, therefore, declared a new capital. Arkansas was now a divided state. Some of its people created a Union government in Little Rock. Others created a Confederate government in Washington, Arkansas. Until the war ended in 1865, Arkansas had two state governments.

The period after the Civil War

was called Reconstruction. During this time, the South should have been rebuilt. The wounds of that bitter war should have been healed. It might have happened if Abraham Lincoln had not been shot. He had always shown great compassion for the people of the South. But he was no longer there to guide the country through this almost impossible task. And Reconstruction became one of the ugliest and most painful eras in American history.

Violence swept the South, including Arkansas. Those who had fought for the Confederacy were often humiliated and deprived of their property and their rights as citizens. The Ku Klux Klan began a reign of terror against blacks and any who dared to help them. It was a terrible time.

During this time, Arkansas was occupied by federal troops. A Republican government was forced upon the state and was in constant struggle with the supporters of the Confederacy. But there were some advances for the people. The University of Arkansas was founded. The state's first system of free public education was adopted. And in 1868, Arkansas approved a new state constitution that gave the vote to black men. Arkansas was readmitted to the Union, but the troops remained.

Then in 1872, Elisha Baxter was elected governor of Arkansas. However, his opponent, another Republican, declared that there had been vote fraud in the election and that he was the real winner. Two years later, this man, Joseph Brooks, took a gun and forced Baxter to leave the Statehouse.

Union troops captured Little Rock in 1863 (left-hand page). In 1874, Elisha Baxter was forced from the governorship by Joseph Brooks (above).

The Arkansas economy in the early 1900s was dependent upon its cotton crop (above).

The people of the state took sides. Fighting broke out in the streets. In 1874, the president of the United States declared that Baxter was governor of Arkansas. He would be the last Republican governor of the state for almost a hundred years.

Also in 1874, the federal troops left Arkansas.

The long-term effects of the war on Arkansas were in some ways worse than the Reconstruction period. The conservative Democrats ruled with an iron hand and managed to take away most of what the black people of the state had gained. The share-cropping system put many blacks and whites on an endless treadmill of terrible poverty. The Arkansas economy was far too dependent on a single crop—cotton.

Well into the twentieth century, the economy developed very, very slowly. There were periods of some prosperity. Between 1870 and 1900, large parts of Arkansas forests and prairies were turned into farms. But in the late 1880s, there was drought as well as a drop in farm prices. Many Arkansas farmers banded together to demand better treatment. They pulled out of the

Democratic Party and worked with labor groups. In 1888, they came close to taking over the government of the state from the Democrats. But the Democrats cheated in the elections, and the rebel farmers rejoined the party in 1900.

At the same time, blacks were pushed out of the voting booth. They were not allowed to join the Democratic party, which meant that they could not vote in the primary elections. And voters were charged a fee, which most blacks could not pay. Many poor whites voted under the orders of the plantation owners for whom they worked.

In the late 1800s, the building of railroads brought work into the state. A valuable mineral called bauxite was discovered near Little Rock, and mining began. Some farmers switched from cotton to rice and soybeans.

In 1921, oil was discovered near El Dorado.

But the Great Depression, which hit all of the United States, came to Arkansas accompanied by terrible droughts. Many farm families became migrant workers, going all over the country wherever they could find work.

But Arkansas made it through the Depression because of new methods of farming and the large public works programs of the Roosevelt administration.

In 1932, Arkansas had a political first. The state elected Hattie Caraway to the United States Senate. She was the first woman ever elected to the U.S. Senate.

World War II brought better times to Arkansas as it did to most of the United States. Industry moved into this once agricultural state. There were more jobs. There were not enough to

An early Arkansas railroad is shown below.

Arkansas Historic Preservation Association

15

Governor Faubus held a press conference in September of 1957, a controversial time in Arkansas.

employ all the farmworkers who had been replaced by machinery, but progress was being made economically.

However, blacks were still being denied their rights including their right to vote. Confrontation was on its way.

In 1954, the Supreme Court of the United States ruled that public schools must be integrated. Black and white children must go to the same schools. Arkansas, like many southern states, did not obey this ruling. The stage was set for Governor Orval E. Faubus.

The court ordered Little Rock's Central High School to integrate in 1957. Governor Faubus resisted and called in the National Guard to prevent it. President Dwight D. Eisenhower put the Guard under federal control and sent in more troops to enforce the integration order. And nine black children walked through screaming mobs to go to school.

Governor Faubus served six consecutive terms.

In 1967, Arkansas elected its first Republican governor since Reconstruction. Governor Winthrop Rockefeller inspired many constructive changes in the state. Under his administration,

Arkansas passed its first real minimum wage law, raised teachers' salaries, and enacted the Arkansas Freedom of Information Law, requiring public groups to allow anyone to see and hear their meetings.

Rockefeller also shut down illegal gambling at Hot Springs, created a code of ethics for **government executives, appointed blacks to important government jobs, and encouraged new** industry to come into the state.

But some say his most important act as governor came the day after Rev. Martin Luther King, Jr.'s assassination. The governor stood on the steps of the state capitol and sang "We Shall Overcome."

In the years that have followed, Arkansas has seen greatly increased economic development, gradual healing of the wounds of racism and segregation, and a new cultural vitality. A beautiful state with great personal and natural resources, Arkansas is coming into its own.

A waterfall on the Cossatot River

Arkansas Department of Parks and Tourism

Rags to Riches

"We was poor sharecroppers, you know. We got up way before daylight and worked 'til dark. So we worked ten to twelve hours every day, you know, six days a week. And the only money we had for clothes or anything is what we worked picking cotton for other people.

"We was always behind in school, and I know that I quit school when I was twelve. That's the way life was back then.

"I'm not working here to get a little richer. I'm here to make a lot of people rich, and poor people not to be poor anymore."

Once upon a time, J.B. Hunt was a truck driver. Now he owns his own trucking company and a whole lot more. J.B. Hunt has been poor, and he has been rich. And there's no question in his mind that rich is better.

That's why J.B. Hunt is trying to make other people rich, starting with the people who work for him.

" . . . I want everybody to be rich. You know, it's like fresh air that I never had before. Now I've got it. Now I want my fellow workers to come on up here and breathe some of this good stuff with me."

J.B. Hunt (foreground) is pictured with two of the many trucks in the J.B. Hunt Transport, Inc. fleet.

18

Photos courtesy J.B. Hunt Transport, Inc.

Photos courtesy J.B. Hunt Transport, Inc.

The atmosphere around Hunt's trucking company shows that Hunt wants more than just to help other people have money. In his company, the workers are treated with respect. They're paid well, yes; but they also have the experience of knowing that the boss is going to say "hi" when he passes them in the hallway. They get advice from the boss about how to invest their money. They have someone paying attention to them and their lives.

"Just paying a guy and you don't care what happens to him is terrible. And I think we have the ability to get these people fired up, get them to work harder, save more, do more, get out there, you know, and do a better job. And everybody wins.

"And that's part of my plan. 'Cause when I die, I should have at least one hundred millionaires working for me—if I live to the age of seventy-five."

J.B. Hunt takes an interest in the well-being of each of his employees (above and opposite).

22

Home

"Well, in my younger days—that went quite a ways back—(we) didn't have much, no extra goodies whatsoever, no electricity. You didn't have meat to put in the refrigerator, so you didn't have refrigerators. Just grin and bear it—or whatever you call it. You had nothing to compare it with, nobody having an easy life there; so you just took it for granted that's what life was about."

As Joe Perme knows, it's a little easier to be poor when you don't know you're poor. And it's easier not having money when you can fish for your dinner in the creek or grow it in your backyard. That's what life was like for a long time in the Ozarks. Everybody was in it together. If you go by what Eul Dean Clark says, everybody still is.

Joe Perme (foreground) and his beautiful Arkansas home (background)

"I know everybody here. I know all about their lives—who they date, who they fuss with, who their friends are and who they don't like, and who they vote for in the elections."

Ponca, Arkansas, the home of Joe and Eul Dean, is one of many Arkansas towns that have changed in only one important way in the last few decades. They're not as poor as they used to be. But when the people who have left (whether it's to live in a nearby town or halfway across the world) return to Ponca for homecoming each October, they still find that they're home.

"They like to come home because they know when they come home, they're loved, and people have thought about them through the years. They all like to get together, and especially they like to come home and eat."

Eat? Do people come from all over the countryside to Ponca just to eat? Are you sure, Eul Dean?

"Well, we have lots of good food—a big roast with potatoes and carrots around it. We have green beans, sweet potatoes, baked beans, lettuce salad, potato salad, macaroni salad, seven layer salad, chicken and dumplings, and chicken and dressing, and ham and roast, and meat loaf, and jello salad,

and cherry supreme salad, pecan, apple, and good old banana pudding, and good apricot cake that Orfee Doody bakes,

and . . ."
Well, maybe they do.

U.S.
POST OFFICE
PONCA, ARK
72670

OPEN WEEKDAYS
7:30 — 4:00
OPEN SATURDAY
8:00

Life from the Land

Life in Arkansas is, and always has been, closely tied to the land. Here, cotton was once king. From plantation owners to sharecropping farmers, the people of Arkansas raised cotton for a living.

Today, agriculture is no longer the state's major economic activity. Most of its people work in factories, stores, and offices. But in Arkansas, even manufacturing depends on the land.

Manufacturing is the leading source of income for the state of Arkansas. And two of the three most important areas of manufacturing are tied directly to the products of its soil. The largest industry is the manufacture of food products. Following it in size is the production of electrical

Food manufacturing is the largest industry in Arkansas. An example is Tyson Manufacturing.

equipment and machinery. And third in importance is the making of lumber and wood products.

This close relationship between the land and the economy is not surprising. More than half of the land in Arkansas is covered with forests. Most of the rest of it is farmland.

There are about fifty-seven thousand farms in the state. Much of the food grown on those farms is processed in the state. In fact, Arkansas factories process about a billion dollars worth of dairy products, canned vege-tables, animal feed, soft drinks, poultry, and rice every year.

The other land-related industry—lumber and wood products—is about half that size. It is the third largest area of manufacturing and accounts for about $400 million in income for the state. Arkansas factories produce everything from raw lumber to finished cabinets.

There is a third industry that falls between these two in size. It is the manufacture of electrical machinery and equipment. Over $900 million worth of air con-

A major Arkansas crop is rice, shown (at left) at harvest time. Sanyo has increased electronics manufacturing in Arkansas (above). Early bauxite mining is pictured (below right).

ditioners, major kitchen appliances, light bulbs, electric motors, and televisions are shipped out of Arkansas factories every year.

Agriculture in Arkansas is pretty evenly divided between crops and livestock. The major crops are soybeans, rice, and cotton. Arkansas is one of America's major producers of rice and cotton.

In livestock, the most important product is chicken. Arkansas raises more broilers—chickens be-tween nine and twelve weeks old —than any other state. And it's one of the country's leading egg producers. Beef cattle are also an important livestock product, as are turkeys, hogs, and dairy cattle.

Two of the state's minerals once played a big part in freeing the economy from its dependence on cotton. They are oil and bauxite. Everyone knows, of course, how valuable oil is for making gasoline and other petroleum products such as plastics. Bauxite is important in making aluminum, which is used in everything from kitchen wrap to space vehicles. Arkansas produces about eighty-five percent of this country's bauxite.

Tourists return each year to Arkansas for its beauty and recreation.

Above is the Marlsgate Plantation. Below right is a view of the famous Hot Springs, Arkansas.

Finally, there are the tourists. Arkansas is a beautiful place with its unspoiled forests and green farms. The visitors who come to enjoy the beauty of Arkansas bring in about a billion and a half dollars every year.

Because people who could not find work could so often live on the land and scrape by somehow, Arkansas was, for a long time, a good place to be poor. Now, with new economic opportunities opening up all over the state, Arkansas has become a good place to stop being poor—for good.

A Farming Family

"Next to my family, I think the soil is my next love. I see that soil as being something precious, something for the future. You know, that dirt's what's going to feed my children and my grandchildren after I'm gone."

Otis Chapman is part of a farming family. That means, of course, that the family makes its living raising food on the farm. But as anyone in this part of the country can tell you, it means a lot more than that, too. It means, for one thing, being the kind of working companions that Otis's sons— Ron and Doug—are.

"Machinery is one of the most orneriest, hardest things in the world to work on. Whenever you get a bearing that won't come off the shaft, tension, tension builds up. You're mad. You just want to take and turn a whole piece of equipment bottom side up. Doug can come in and say, you know, 'Let me have it. I see what you're doing wrong.' And I turn it over to him, and the thing just slips right off. I don't know. It's just something there that, whenever he gets a victory, I get a victory. Whenever something goes good for him, it's going good for me."

Being part of a farm family means other things, as well, especially these days. Times are hard

The Chapmans prepare their land for herbicide treatment (below). Below right is Otis Chapman.

Photos courtesy Chapman Bros. Farms

33

for the American farmer. Every year, more small, family farms close down. The farmers have to leave and go to the city to find work. But they often take their values with them.

"Even if we did quit farming, if we went out and had to knock on doors trying to sell something, anything— vacuum cleaners, encyclopedias, shoes, Tupperware—we'd get into a partnership. The two of us, we know what the other is going to do or what he's capable of doing. And what one of us can't do, the other one can. And if he can't do it, he's willing to try."

The Chapmans hope they will never have to leave the farm. And they hope not only for themselves but for the land, too.

"It's really hard to say. I don't believe the countryside would even look right without us being around here. It needs someone like us, just like we need it—

Doug, Ron, and Otis Chapman load fence posts onto a trailer (below).

Photos courtesy Chapman Bros. Farms

34

somebody to take care of it, and watch over it, and maintain it."

That's what farmland has always needed—farm families.

Grain is transferred on the Chapman farm (right). Otis Chapman sprays herbicide on a field (below).

Far from the Plantation

Arkansas has seen many different ways of life from the ancient but advanced civilizations of the Bluff Dwellers and Mound Builders to the slavery-bound plantation society to the painful poverty of the tenant farmers. Today, the people of Arkansas hold onto the good things of many of those cultures.

In the small towns of rural Arkansas, there is a culture that in many ways grew out of poverty. Here, the community was once all important to people (black and white) who could not hope to survive alone. Today, community activities remain an important part of life. The people of rural Arkansas eat together, dance together, and sing together. They entertain each other, creating art that costs nothing

and gives a great deal.

One showplace for this kind of art is the Arkansas Folk Festival held every year at Mountain View. But for the most part, folk art is created not to be displayed in museums or heard on recordings, but to be enjoyed by the neighbors.

The Arkansas Arts Center in Little Rock opened in 1963. The Arts Center, along with other arts organizations such as the Arkansas Symphony Orchestra and the Bach Society, is part of a move to improve the quality of life in Arkansas. This move is supported by the Industrial Development Commission of the state in hopes that new industry will be attracted to the state.

Any picture of life in Arkansas must take into consideration that this is a state that once fought fiercely to keep its black and white people apart.

For a long time, there were really two cultures in Arkansas, the black and the white. In the days of the plantations, of course, the differences between the two ways of life were striking and horrible. The gracious life of the white owner was bought at the cost of poverty, pain, and often death for the black slave.

Later, poverty was the lot of both black and white in the state. But the two races remained rigidly separate.

Today, in Arkansas, that has begun to change.

Musicians perform at the Mountain View Folk Festival (above). At right: the Arkansas Art Center (top), the parade at the Folk Festival (left), and a performance by the Arkansas Symphony Orchestra (right).

Little Rock Central High

"When my family heard that I had decided to come to Arkansas, they had a fit."

And who can blame them? Marie McNeil was a young black woman from Harlem in New York City. Little Rock, Arkansas, was the town where, in 1957, government troops were called out to escort the first black students into Central High. Why would Marie McNeil bring her education and her enthusiasm here? Maybe because this is where they were needed.

"When people think of Arkansas, we're last in everything. If not last, we're forty-ninth. Sometimes I feel Arkansas has been degraded so much that there are many people in our state who don't have high hopes for us."

If Marie McNeil has anything to say about it, those people will not be the students in her classroom. It is part of her mission as a teacher to give her students pride in themselves and in their state. And that pride begins with freeing themselves from the past.

"People still think of Arkansas as Little Rock Central, 1957. I think it has affected a lot of students at times. We constantly see people driving up in front of the school, taking pictures, and thinking, 'Well, I wonder what it was like in 1957.' Little Rock Central is not like 1957."

One look will tell you that. Here are black and white faces in the same classroom looking up at the same teacher. Here are blacks and whites playing together on

Little Rock Convention and Visitors Bureau

the football field and singing the same school song together. This is not like 1957.

And Marie McNeil is sure that her students will take Arkansas further in the future.

"You feel good about yourself, right? You reside in the state of Arkansas. Put the two together. What makes your state so great? What elements make Arkansas first? Where is her greatness? (Student: The people.) *Who said that? Did you hear what he said? Say it again. Come on. The people! In the people! You will make Arkansas better than what she is now."*

Marie McNeil is pictured against a photo of Little Rock Central High School.

Tomorrow in Arkansas

An interesting thing has happened in the United States. There is a small group of states that people in other parts of the country have sometimes thought of as backward. Progress seemed to pass them by. In other states, factories dotted the countryside and skyscrapers carved out the city skylines. But these states, well, these states seemed to remain somehow in the past.

And then an interesting thing happened. The people in the prosperous, progressive states began to look around. They began to see what they had lost. Those factories that had once promised the good life now looked ugly crouching on the horizon. The trees that were cut and the streams that were dirtied to make the factories run were missed now. The

"The Old Mill" in North Little Rock

small communities broken apart by the demands of modern business and industry could not be rebuilt.

And the handful of states that had once looked "backward," now looked very beautiful.

Arkansas has many problems as it goes into the last part of the twentieth century. There is still too much poverty. Tax income is not really enough to support state services. Badly needed reforms in the state constitution have been turned down by the voters.

On the other hand, Arkansas is in a wonderful position. With so much of its beauty unspoiled and so many of its people holding to solid values long lost in more industrial states, Arkansas gets to pick and choose what it will keep from the past as it goes into the future. It can learn from the mistakes made by some of the more progressive states. Arkansas still has what many of those states have lost forever. And it has the chance to carry the good things from its past proudly into its future.

Important Historical Events in Arkansas

1541 Spanish explorer Hernando de Soto is the first European to enter the Arkansas area.

1673 Marquette and Jolliet come down the Mississippi from Canada.

1682 La Salle claims the entire Mississippi Valley including Arkansas for France, calling it the Louisiana Territory.

1686 De Tonti builds a camp at the mouth of the Arkansas River.

1763 Spain gains control of the Louisiana Territory.

1800 France regains the Louisiana Territory.

1803 Louisiana Purchase. Thomas Jefferson buys the Louisiana Territory for the United States.

1812 The state of Louisiana is formed. The rest of the Louisiana Purchase land becomes the Missouri Territory.

1819 What is now Arkansas and part of Oklahoma becomes the Arkansas Territory.

1836 Arkansas becomes a state.

1861 The Civil War begins. Arkansas withdraws from the Union.

1864 A Union government is set up in part of Arkansas.

1868 Arkansas is readmitted to the Union.

1874 The present state constitution is adopted.

1887 Bauxite is discovered near Little Rock.

1921 Oil is discovered near El Dorado.

1924 First hydroelectric dam in Arkansas is built near Malvern.

1932 Hattie Caraway becomes the first woman to be elected to the United States Senate.

1957 Federal troops are sent in to enforce integration of Central High School in Little Rock.

1966 Winthrop Rockefeller becomes first Republican governor of Arkansas since Reconstruction.

1970 The Arkansas River Development Program opens the river to navigation from the Mississippi to Oklahoma.

1980 Arkansas rejects a new constitution.

Arkansas Almanac

Nickname. The Land of Opportunity.

Capital. Little Rock.

State Bird. Mockingbird.

State Flower. Apple blossom.

State Tree. Pine tree.

State Motto. *Regnat Populus* (The People Rule).

State Song. Arkansas.

State Abbreviations. Ark. (traditional); AR (postal).

Statehood. June 15, 1836, the 25th state.

Government. Congress: U.S. senators, 2; U.S. representatives 4. **State Legislature:** senators, 35; representatives, 100. **Counties:** 75.

Area. 53,104 sq. mi. (137,539 sq. km.) 27th in size among the states.

Greatest Distances. north/south, 240 mi. (386 km.); east/west, 275 mi. (443 km.).

Elevation. Highest: Magazine Mountain, 2,753 ft. (839 m). **Lowest:** 55 ft. (17 m), along the Ouachita River.

Population. 1980 Census: 2,285,513 (19% increase over 1970), 33rd among the states. **Density:** 43 persons per sq. mi. (17 persons per sq. km.). **Distribution:** 52% urban, 48% rural. **1970 Census:** 1,923,322.

Economy. Agriculture: beef cattle, broilers, soybeans, cotton, rice, hay, wheat, sorghum, tomatoes, peaches, strawberries. **Manufacturing:** food products, poultry products, forestry products, home appliances, aluminum, electric motors, transformers, clothing, bricks, fertilizer, petroleum products, fabricated metal products, printed materials. **Mining:** bauxite, petroleum, natural gas, bromine, stone, sand and gravel.

Places to Visit

Blanchard Springs Caverns, near Mountain View.

Crater of Diamonds, near Murfreesboro.

Dogpatch, U.S.A., near Harrison.

Hot Springs National Park.

Magnet Cave, near Hot Springs.

Ozark Folk Center in Mountain View.

Pea Ridge National Military Park.

The Plantation Museum in Scott.

Annual Events

Arkansas Folk Festival and Ozark Foothills Handicraft Show in Mountain View (April).

Arkansas State Festival of the Arts in Little Rock (May).

Quapaw Quarter Tour in Little Rock (May).

Four States Fair and Rodeo in Texarcana (September).

Arkansas State Fair and Livestock Show in Little Rock (September-October).

Ozark Frontier Trail Festival and Craft Show in Heber Springs (October).

Arts, Crafts, and Design Fair in Little Rock (November).

Arkansas Counties

INDEX